Oh GORD!

The Funniest Gordon Strachan Quotes

by Gordon Law

Printed in Europe and the USA
ISBN: 9781701891210
Imprint: Independently published

Photo courtesy of: Tomasz Bidermann/Shutterstock.com

Contents

Introduction

There are few people in football who can light up a press conference in a way the witty Gordon Strachan can.

The Scotsman can always be trusted to come out with a funny sound bite or sarcastic quip whenever he is thrust in front of the media.

By avoiding football's stock phrases or dull cliches, Strachan is a journalist's dream... or nightmare.

A master at swerving difficult questions, he was once asked for a quick word after a defeat and replied with "velocity" before walking off.

He also claimed he was more worried about the expiry date on his yoghurt than discuss his Southampton striker Agustin Delgado.

And when a reporter said he didn't take losing lightly, a sharp Strachan responded, "I don't take stupid comments lightly either."

He has blamed Scotland's short players for failing to qualify for the World Cup and even bemoaned the sweat patches on his shirt due to high-pressure games.

When Strachan is not ranting on the touchline, he is just as entertaining in his work as a TV pundit. Whether it's handing out a tongue lashing to players or taking a swipe at the England team, he's always great value.

Many of Strachan's weird and wonderful observations can be found here in this unique collection of quotations. Enjoy!

Gordon Law

OH GORD!

CALL THE MANAGER

"If you get a lot of chances and miss them then there is nothing you can do. It's human error. There's no way I can come in at the end of the game and stick bamboo shoots up the fingernails for missing chances."

Gordon Strachan after a goalless draw in Celtic's season opener against Kilmarnock

Journalist: "Is that your best start to a season?"

Strachan: "Well, I've still got a job so it's far better than the Coventry one, that's for sure."

The Southampton boss after watching his first game. Strachan had departed Coventry just five games into the season

"I don't know how you face people after that. When you go and speak to your mates and they ask what did you contribute to the game and you say, 'I fell, I fell like a big Jessie'."

His verdict on Bolton's Mario Jardel

"If he did jump into the crowd, then the referee had to book him. I can't tell the players before a game that, if they score, they shouldn't jump into the crowd. If my hip was a bit better, I'd have been in there as well."

After Jan Vennegoor of Hesselink's stoppage-time winner against Inverness earned him a second yellow card

"At Falkirk the other week, the police were asked to speak to me about smiling at the crowd. Someone reported me for smiling in his direction. Obviously it's not the best smile in the world. I can see a lot better smiles, but I never knew my smile could be offensive, but there you go. That's the world we live in just now."

The Celtic manager on a complaint from a supporter

"Paul told me that's the first one he's missed, which I find very surprising having seen that."

On Paul Hartley's penalty against Hearts

"I just told them – it's not your pitch anyway."

To the Fulham fans after they spotted him out of his technical area

"[Fabien] Barthez sat in my office smoking during the second half. He comes off for ill health and puts a fag in his mouth. Is that not ironic? It's a no-smoking area too."

The Saints boss after the Manchester United keeper was substituted

"There's a lot of ice in that dressing room – it's like the dining room on the Titanic in there."

After Celtic's physical game at Hearts

Journalist: "What areas did you think Middlesbrough were superior in?"

Strachan: "That big grassy one out there for a start."

The Scot is ramping up the sarcasm after a Southampton defeat

Reporter: "Gordon, tell us how you're feeling winning back-to-back titles here today."

Strachan: "Sorry I cannot describe my position to anybody... I'd love to but... I've never taken drugs but I wonder if it's a bit like this!"

On clinching the title with Celtic after a stoppage-time winner against Kilmarnock

"I never see anything, I'm like the fourth official, I never see anything at any time."

The Celtic boss after a fan went onto the pitch against AC Milan

"I was in shock afterwards. It was like being in a car crash, getting a bump and then thinking you're OK. It's 10 minutes later when you start shaking, and that's a bit how I felt."

On Coventry's 5-1 home loss to Newcastle

"Minging."

His view of Southampton's 0-0 at Bolton

"When we put him on the coach we'll have to make sure he's still got all his arms and legs. I'm sure one or two bits of him are still left out there."

After Coventry's Darren Huckerby felt the full force of a rough Chelsea side

"What annoys me is when a policewoman tells me to sit down, as happened at Everton. Or a steward, or a linesman who should be watching the game, a referee, likewise. The only person who should be saying anything is the fourth official."

The Coventry boss is annoyed with the cops

"We were good going forward but in defence
we were like my art at school – we are going
backward and not very good."
The Celtic manager on his back line

"I was watching some golf this morning and
that was as good a swing as I have seen all
day."
**On an ungainly Carlton Palmer getting sent
off for fighting**

"We were disappointed at being so excited."
**On celebrating Coventry avoiding
relegation**

"When we were going to put Roy [Keane] on he disappeared to the toilet."

The Celtic chief couldn't find his sub

"It was clearly a case of sour grapes on the part of a few sad characters who must have nothing better to do with their lives."

The Coventry manager was reported for swearing by Southampton fans

"You talk about sexy football – that was more like perversity."

On Coventry's dull encounter with Sheffield Wednesday

"I don't believe it. There must be a rule that says we don't go through. I will wake up tomorrow and find someone has scored an extra goal against us somewhere. I better check Teletext tomorrow to make sure."

After a 1-0 win over Man United took Celtic into the Champions League knockout stage

"The whole thing was an embarrassment to everyone at the club. That includes players who were not playing. If they are not good enough to get picked for that, they really must be embarrassed."

Strachan following another Coventry defeat

OH GORD!

PLAYER POWER

"Someone said to me after the match, 'Will you drop him for the next game?'. I was laughing but realised he was serious and then he actually said, 'Are you going to take sanctions?' I didn't know he was a country or was president of Iran. Now we have to stop food parcels getting through to his house! There won't be any sanctions against Artur."

On Celtic goalie Artur Boruc's poor display

"He can be a miserable sod when he's not playing. He's like the Grim Reaper walking about the ground, so it's nice to see him back playing."

On his Celtic striker Craig Beattie

"You are really going mental when you are having arguments with people who are not even here."

The Celtic boss on rumours he had a row with Paul Telfer who had left a month earlier

"I've told him there is always room for bald, grumpy old men in my team."

Chris Marsden still has a Saints future

"Unlike most defenders, who like the ball up the other end of the pitch, he prefers when it is in our penalty box because he loves defending. And playing for Coventry he'll have plenty of defending to do."

On new Coventry signing Mohammed Konjic

"Scott McDonald, the most intelligent man in the world, Stephen Hawking him. He knows everything. Every time you tell him something, he knows it, done it, seen it, been it, that's why we call him Stephen Hawking. That man can do anything!"

The manager on his Celtic player

"[Agustin] Delgado comes alive every two years or so."

The Southampton boss takes a swipe

"It is a strange decision, but then he is a strange person."

On Chris Marsden joining Busan Icons

"He never shuts up. He talks some rubbish, but we throw that away and sometimes some intelligence comes out."

The Scotsman on Carlton Palmer

Journalist: "What qualities will Jan Vennegoor of Hesselink bring?"

Gordon Strachan: "I have no idea, but I said I'd bring a big name to the club."

"He is not a bad lad. If he said, 'God bless Myra Hindley', I might have a problem."

After Artur Boruc wound up Rangers fans by wearing a 'God Bless the Pope' t-shirt

"When he was carried off at Leicester someone asked me if he was unconscious, but I didn't have a clue. He's always like that."

On Saints star Claus Lundekvam

"Whatever I say, I feel like I'm the commandant in The Great Escape and you're Steve McQueen. You're always trying to escape, but I'm always trying to bring you back!"

On handling Celtic keeper Artur Boruc

"[Marians] Pahars has also caught every virus going except a computer virus and he is probably working on that even now."

On his player's poor fitness record

"Neil Lennon has a hamstring strain. Paul Telfer is injured too – why are there no rumours about Paul Telfer? The poor guy gets ignored all the time. He just wants one rumour."

Strachan wants some love for Telfer

"Robbie is very special to us. I'm just hoping Robbie doesn't like the San Siro, doesn't like the wages and wants to come back here."

On Robbie Keane's transfer from Coventry to Inter Milan

"5ft 10in, size 10 feet, as elegant as footballers get; totally different to me, in other words."

The Coventry boss on his son Gavin

OH GORD!

CAN YOU MANAGE?

"The only thing certain for a manager is that he will be sacked. How do you think my family would feel if I'd ignored them for 25 years? Do you think they'd be happy if having not seen them for all that time I arrived home after being sacked and said, 'Hi, I'm back'."

Strachan on the perils of management

"I have discovered that when you go to Anfield or Old Trafford, it pays not to wear a coloured shirt because everyone can see the stains as the pressure mounts. I always wear a white shirt so nobody sees you sweat."

On coping with pressure

"The world looks a totally different place after two wins. I can even enjoy watching Blind Date or laugh at Noel's House Party."

The manager enjoys watching the box

"If you're obsessed with winning and you don't do it, you end up a lunatic."

In his early days at Coventry

"I tried to get the disappointment out of my system by going for a walk. I ended up 17 miles from home and I had to phone my wife Lesley to come and pick me up."

Strachan finds defeat hard to accept

OH GORD!

"No one, unless they manage a team, can know how I feel. No one, not an assistant manager, a player, anyone. They haven't a clue."

After Coventry lose out to Middlesbrough

"The first game I went to after being sacked by Coventry was at Rushden and Diamonds. I didn't want any fuss so I put a hat on to cover my hair, but one bloke said, 'Look at his nose! It's Gordon Strachan'."

The Scot stands out in a crowd

"If you can manage Celtic, you can be prime minister."

On the pressure of managing the club

"People don't understand a manager wanting to spend more time with his wife and family. Do I wait until people are screaming at me, my wife is going off her head and I'm a nervous wreck? I love football, but it's not an obsession."
An unemployed Strachan, shortly before joining Celtic

"My mum and dad had a word with me about it so I had a check-up a few weeks ago and I'm a perfectly formed specimen. Very relaxed."
Strachan said his parents wanted him to see a doctor after his emotional outbursts on the Coventry touchline

"You have to get used to the pressure. There
is no release unless you are a Buddhist monk
and you meditate, they tell me that works well.
I've got a local pub I go to on a Saturday night
at about 9.30pm. Everybody there is not
interested in football. You go and talk about
who is doing what in the village."
**The Celtic manager likes to escape the
goldfish bowl**

"Just like 17 per cent of us have ginger hair,
a lot of us Scots are small. You could build up
a hugely talented Celtic side and Snow White
would have to lead them out because there are
so many small people here."
On the genetics of Scotland

"It can do silly things to you, obsession. If you're obsessive and if you don't get to the point you want to achieve you can become a basket case. I've seen loads of them."

The Coventry boss on commitment

"In my office, I often regret the fact that players do not sit in chairs fitted with a lie detector and an ejector seat."

His Saints stars have been sinners

"It's a great day for me to do this and it's been 40 years in the making."

Strachan somehow predicted he'd become Scotland manager

"This is no use to me because I don't drink coffee. Where I come from in the Muirhouse district in Edinburgh, no one was brought up to drink coffee."

After Celtic's tea bag supply was confiscated by US customs on their pre-season tour

"I never wanted to be a manager, I wanted to be a coach. But to have the power of coaching, you've got to be the manager because the manager tells you how to coach. So the only reason I'm a manager is to be a coach."

The Saints boss enjoys spending time on the training ground

"Sometimes he phones me when he sees a couple of results haven't gone my way. When I ring he always says, 'Where are you?' I reply, 'I'm just on the edge of a cliff, in my car'. If we've had a poor run, I make a bubbling sound, and tell him, 'I've gone over. I'm in the water now'."

On his phone chats with Howard Wilkinson during his time at Coventry

Q: "Who is your closest friend at the club?"

A: "I am the manager. I have no friends."

From the Coventry programme

"I took a pay cut to come here. As long as the fridge is full, I'm happy."

On joining Coventry as player-coach from Leeds

"I don't know. I'll have to see where easyJet are going."

When asked what his plans are after leaving Southampton

"If you don't know what's going on, start waving your arms about as if you do."

The Saints boss on his dug-out antics

"I'm like a dad to my players, mixing small tellings-off with a lot of love."

On dealing with his Coventry squad

Journalist: "Welcome to Southampton. Do you think you're the right man to turn things around?"

Strachan: "No. I was asked whether I thought I was the right man for the job and I said, 'No, I think they should have got George Graham because I'm useless'."

His first press conference as Southampton manager

OH GORD!

MEDIA CIRCUS

OH GORD!

Reporter: "Where will Marion Pahars fit into the team line-up?"

Strachan: "Not telling you! It's a secret."

"We're not doing bad. What do you expect us to be like? We were eighth in the league last year, in the cup final and we got into Europe. I don't know where you expect me to get to. Do you expect us to win the Champions League?"

Strachan is irked by a journalist's question

"That'll be the Samaritans. They usually call me this time of day."

After a phone rang during a Saints press conference

Journalist: "So, Gordon, any plans for Europe this year?"

Strachan: "Aye, me and the wife quite fancy Spain in August."

"You people sometimes are like those serial killers you see in films who send out these horrible messages. The serial killer who cuts out the words 'I'm going to get you' or 'Your wife is next'. You are the very same."

Strachan on the Scottish media

Interviewer: "What is your impression of Jermaine Pennant?"

Strachan: "I don't do impressions."

Reporter: "Gordon, a clean sheet... it's been a while since you managed to say that?"

Celtic's Strachan: "Aye... I was about 15."

Q: "There's no negative vibes or negative feelings here?"

A: "Apart from yourself, we're all quite positive round here. I'm going to whack you over the head with a big stick. Down, negative man, down."

Journalist: "Gordon, can we have a quick word please?"

Strachan: "Velocity."

"Oh, no, no, no, no. I'm not going to sit here and answer questions from members of the public. They can do it themselves. You think it's a hotline here? It's like I'm on Radio Clyde on a Saturday night. For goodness sake! No, you're not getting any now because they're coming for other people. You'll have to think about your own ones. Right, anybody else?"

The Scotland chief tells a journalist he doesn't want questions from fans

"Tell Rodney to get a f*cking move on! Or I'm off! Where's Rodney?"

The Scotland manager gets agitated with a Maltese interviewer while waiting to go live

"The media coverage for Tommy [Burns] over the last few days has been fantastic, even the half-wit on Real Radio was quite good."
The Celtic boss has a dig at the local station

Interviewer: "When it's 1-0, do you always feel there is a chance of getting back in it?"
The Saints chief: "Yes. When it's 5-0 I always feel there's no chance of getting back in it. Thank you for stating the obvious there. That was wonderful."

Reporter: "So Gordon, any changes then?"
Strachan: "Naw, still 5ft 6in, ginger and a big nose."

"I've got more important things to think about. I've got a yoghurt to finish by today. The expiry date is today. That can be my priority rather than Agustin Delgado."

When asked about his Southampton striker

"One or two 'voices of football' – I've been told – said that we played 4-5-1. That was terrific to work out because I never worked that out. You must be better geniuses than me. I must be really ordinary because I sent out a 4-4-2. If you saw something else then that was fantastic. I was wasting my time getting my badges – I should have just joined a radio station."

Mocking the press after Celtic clinch the League Cup

"People think I've got a problem with the press. Actually I have no problem with the press. But just like in football there are a handful who cause problems because they're disrespectful, they're lazy, and above all – and this is what really gets to me – they haven't worked hard to get there."

Maybe Strachan does have a problem

"Journalism now is dominated by yob culture. I've seen it creeping in during the last three or four years. You get papers now printing s-dot-dot-dot and w-asterisk-asterisk-asterisk-asterisk-asterisk. That never happened when I played."

The Coventry boss on the state of the media

"What you should ask is who is posing the question? Not an intelligent person, that's for sure. It's someone who's sitting with his tracksuit on, his devil dug at his side and a can of Kestrel in his hand, maybe coked up to his eyeballs, shouting down the phone. I'm not answering to that. I'm not answering a question from Mr Ned."

The Celtic manager when asked about the pressure of Champions League qualifiers

Saints boss Strachan: "We were boring if I'm honest with you. Totally and utterly boring."

Reporter: "What do you put that down to?"

Strachan: "Boring football."

Reporter: "This might sound like a daft question, but you'll be happy to get your first win under your belt, won't you?"

Strachan: "You're right. It is a daft question. I'm not even going to bother answering that one. It is a daft question, you're spot on there."

"Really? The boy who played today then was better than Artur Boruc. What a great place this new training academy is. We are cloning players now. Now that we have two, maybe I can sell one and keep the other."

After a journalist said he heard the keeper did not train with the squad

"If I put Riordan in instead of Nakamura, you're off your head; take Aiden out, you're off your head; leave Maciej out, you're off your head. So basically, I'm off my head."

He says the media will never be happy with the side he picks

Reporter: "You don't take losing lightly, do you Gordon?"

Strachan: "I don't take stupid comments lightly either."

"Britain's Got Talent is absolutely fantastic – the funniest thing on TV. I can't wait to get home."

The Celtic boss to the assembled media

"Well, not if you and I keep talking about it."

When asked if a change of Celtic's tactics would surprise opponents Spartak

"Trying to explain it to you would be impossible. It would be like you trying to explain childbirth to me."

Celtic's manager to a (childless) female reporter who asked for his view on a defeat

"Christ, you're everywhere. You're like dogsh*t."

The Celtic boss to a journalist who sat in with the TV and radio people, the daily newspapers and then the Sunday ones

Journalist: "Gordon, you must be delighted with that result."

Strachan: "Spot on. You can read me like a book."

After a Southampton victory

"Fans can be easily manipulated by you. You can start wars you people, never mind going for managers."

The Celtic boss takes aim at the reporters

Journalist: "What was your impression of Leeds?"

Strachan: "I don't do impressions."

After a Southampton draw away at Leeds

Journalist: "Bang, there goes your unbeaten run. Can you take it?"

Strachan: "No, I'm just going to crumble like a wreck. I'll go home, become an alcoholic and maybe jump off a bridge. Um, I think I can take it, yeah."

"I just needed a [summer] break. Like I said I don't have a problem with the players speaking, but I'd imagine that most newspaper guys needed a break from me as well!"

The Celtic boss ahead of the close season

"Honestly, I've had more trouble with blackheads."

He downplays John Hartson's knee injury

Reporter: "How does it feel to be back managing where it all began all those years ago?"

Gordon Strachan: "Old."

Before a return to his old club Dundee

Journalist: "Do you think James Beattie deserves to be in the England squad?"

Strachan: "I don't care, I'm Scottish."

"When he talks about the happiest incidents, like a birthday or a grandchild, he makes it sound like the most depressing thing you've heard in your life."

On his Match of the Day colleague Alan Hansen

OH GORD!

FIELD OF DREAMS

"He used to come round your house on a Friday night. You seen his car sneaking by on a Friday night, seeing if you were in. What a sad man – on a Friday night sneaking about in his car to see if I was in."

On playing under Alex Ferguson

"I would love to see the FA, PFA and all the Premiership clubs get together and pay Forest the £4m they spent on Van Hooijdonk. Then we would tell Forest, 'Use that money and leave Van Hooijdonk to rot'. It would be good for the whole of football because we would be making an example of this man."

The Coventry boss on the Dutch forward who went on strike

"I asked for a transfer myself in 1982 when I handed Alex Ferguson a request and was told to go forth and multiply."

Looking back on his time at Aberdeen

"He used to do a lot of scouting in places like Florida, the Bahamas and Barbados but, funny, he never got us any players from there."

On Coventry manager Ron Atkinson

"Football is about what happens in the two penalty areas. Everything else is propaganda."

The Saints boss on the beautiful game

"When I see Alex, I'm always civil, but there's no exchange of Christmas cards. His book should have been a celebration of his achievements, something positive, but he chose to use it as something else. He had a different agenda."
After being slated by Alex Ferguson in his first autobiography

"He has a different language to that of most English-speaking people. I think he tries out some of his expressions on us before using them on television. I remember him announcing that a particular full-back was 'getable'. I told him it wasn't a word."
The player-coach on his Coventry manager Ron Atkinson

"It's an incredible rise to stardom; at 17 you're more likely to get a call from Michael Jackson than Sven-Goran Eriksson."

Strachan on Wayne Rooney

"Arsene Wenger has a machine gun, Tony Mowbray has a water pistol."

On the differences in resources between Arsenal and Celtic

Gary Lineker: "So Gordon, if you were English, what formation would you play?"

Gordon Strachan: "If I was English, I'd top myself."

The TV pundit at the 2006 World Cup

"Once people left Manchester United, everyone used to think you went away, curled up and died... I didn't fancy that, dying a death at 32."
Strachan on departing for Leeds

"If you're dribbling and you keep getting kicked in the shins you say, 'I think it's about time I passed now'. That's the way you learn. Not by people shouting at you about offside when you're nine. That's nonsense."
The Coventry manager's advice to kids

"Fergie is driven by anger. It's like petrol to him."
Strachan on Alex Ferguson

"If he'd run that fast after Kaka in 2007 we'd have got to the quarter-finals of the Champions League!"

He compares Neil Lennon's Dundee victory celebrations to Celtic's defeat to AC Milan

"I always felt there's a scriptwriter up on a cloud somewhere penning Kenny's life story."

On Dalglish's title victory with Blackburn

"They say an unmade bed is art. But what Zidane does, that's art."

Working as a pundit at Euro 2004

"No one coached me before I was 14 or 15. Before that I could fantasise about being Jimmy Johnstone, Peter Marinello, Pat Stanton or Colin Stein. There was no one trying to organise me. I could run all over the field and play in every position. Now we tell eight-year-old kids they are a right back."

The Coventry boss on educating youngsters

"Sometimes driving home from a game, you do wonder if you're getting a bit old. But I always remember what Kenny Dalglish once told me, 'Never forget that football made you feel knack-ered when you were 17'."

The veteran midfielder at Leeds

"There were a lot of nasty moments, too, like the time Fergie threatened to dismember us after only beating Rangers 1-0 in the 1983 final. He meant dismember the team, but at the time a lot of us thought he meant each of us, piece by piece."

On winning the Scottish Cup with Aberdeen

"He used to play tapes of a singer he liked – I don't know who it was but it was crap. All the boys hated it, until one night it got chucked away. If he's still wondering who threw it off the bus, it was me. So maybe he was right and I'm not to be trusted."

On Alex Ferguson's choice of music on the team bus

"We Scots don't mind laughing at ourselves. But it's getting to the stage where other people are laughing at us."

Strachan on the Scotland side of 2004

"For three weeks [the other players] thought I was lying. I'd made out he was Hannibal Lecter and he'd been a pussycat. Then we lost at Wimbledon..."

On Alex Ferguson's early days at United

"My bum has been through every temperature known to man."

The Leeds player on the various heating and freezing treatments

"If a Frenchman goes on about seagulls, trawlers and sardines, he's called a philosopher. I'd just be called a short Scottish bum talking cr*p."

He responds to Eric Cantona's famous quote

"We owe the English big time. They stole our land, our oil, perpetrated the Highland Clearances and now they've even pinched Billy Connolly."

Ahead of Scotland's Euro 2000 play-off with England

"It's a tremendous honour. I'm going to have a banana to celebrate."

After being named 1991 Footballer of the Year

"These are people with no friends... who spend 10 hours a day on the internet and have no one to talk to. The internet is a powerful tool. People are bringing down the government in Egypt by going on the internet, so it can be used for good. But three or four abusive idiots on a football message board do not speak for the majority."
Strachan slams the keyboard warriors

"Just as well you've not got a touch like Bobo Balde or you'd go straight through that window."
The Celtic boss to motor neurone disease patient Jimmy Johnstone after he controlled his wheelchair with his foot

"The kids came through from the swimming pool and said that Leeds had signed Vinnie Jones. I started laughing and they said no, it was serious. I leapt into the pool, but thought, 'There's no point in drowning yourself, you're getting well paid'."

Strachan was shocked at the new signing

"What I do know is that genetically we are behind. In the last campaign we were the second smallest squad behind Spain. Genetically we have to work at things. It is a problem for us."

The Scotland manager puts an unusual spin on his side's struggles

OH GORD!

REF
JUSTICE

"If I have been sent off for looking like a strange wee man, then I can't appeal against that. If he has sent me to the stand because I'm only 5ft 5in, then I can't argue with that... But until I find out what he sent me to the stand for, then it has to be a problem."

He is baffled as to why he was sent from the dugout against Hearts

"The referee was a joke, an absolute disgrace, and the FA can come after me if they want."

The Coventry boss on Stephen Lodge's display during the 2-2 draw with Arsenal

"We are now getting PC decisions about promoting ladies. It does not matter whether they are ladies, men or Alsatian dogs. If they are not good enough to run the line then they should not get the job."

After assistant referee Wendy Toms failed to flag for an offside for his Coventry team

"Maybe the small bloke with the ginger hair and the big nose stood out a bit."

On how referees can't miss him in the Coventry dugout

"I tried to talk to the ref but it's easier to get an audience with the Pope. If I'm in London again and I get mugged, I hope the same amount of people turn up. There were six police officers, four stewards and a UN peace-keeping observer."

The Southampton manager after their game with Arsenal

"My players wouldn't take a throw-in for that sort of money."

On hearing that referee Gerald Ashby's match fee was £20 in 1998

"There's no point in asking a referee for an explanation of his action. You get that in the report a couple of weeks later, when everyone has got the right story. The boys in black have time to organise a story, make sure it's right and then send it out. Yet I have to try to give instant explanations."

After Coventry were defeated by Liverpool

"Maybe I scored a goal against his favourite team 30 years ago."

The Celtic boss on referee Stuart Dougal who sent him to the stand

OH GORD!

LIFESTYLE CHOICE

"He used to nick my bacon sandwiches. I was always hungry and I was always eating garbage. He used to hijack my food. He would sit down near the bar of our hotel and watch for room service coming. He'd ask the waiter, 'Where are they going?' Mr Strachan ordered them, sir? 'No son, they're for me now'. I used to ring up and say, 'Where's my sandwiches?'. They'd say, 'Mr Stein had them'."

On the then-Scotland manager Jock Stein

"Going out drinking doesn't help team spirit. When you drink, you just tell lies and talk rubbish."

Strachan on the downsides of boozing

"I won't say I'll definitely pick Gavin until he does something about his room. It's a real tip and it's driving his mum crazy."

On giving son Gavin his debut for Coventry

"Right, that's me sorted. Can of Coca-Cola, packet of crisps and three hours watching the table on Teletext."

After Southampton moved up to fourth in the Premier League

"I switch off by sitting in the house watching telly. I watch all the garbage, Family Fortunes, things like that."

The Coventry boss loves the game show

OH GORD!

"I take my wife Lesley to watch midweek matches. She's in the studio audience tonight. It's one of the rare times I've taken her out somewhere she doesn't need to wear an overcoat."

The Saints manager on the BBC programme 'Onside'

"People say he lived life to the full on and off the pitch. Unfortunately, I lived life to the full with him just one day. We went out drinking in Dundee and my liver is still recovering. My wife didn't speak to me for a week, but it was great fun."

He hails Celtic great Jimmy Johnstone

"I didn't know the witch had been there but she can take training for the next two weeks so I can practice my golf."

On the pagan witch who attempted to lift the curse on St Mary's Stadium

"I've had better weeks. I tried to make it better by playing my dad at golf on Sunday. We played 13 holes and I got beat by a 60-year-old man with a bad limp. So hopefully bad things happen in threes and that will be the last of it."

After Celtic missed out on qualifying for the Champions League, despite beating Artmedia Bratislava 4-0

OH GORD!

"All this 'breathe in and stabilise' stuff – the instructor never told us to breathe out again. So for two minutes, I was holding my breath. I nearly killed myself."

On taking pilates classes after departing Middlesbrough

"[He's] living with his granny, eating at home and his uncles are there to look after him. And I've no worries about his mental strength. He made his debut against Aston Villa in the cup, where Coventry hadn't won in a hundred years, ended up on the winning side, and didn't bat an eyelid."

The Coventry boss on his son Gavin

"At least they are still eating properly – taking their bananas and proteins. Total professionals."

After Jiri Jarosik was pictured in a tabloid holding a banana in a seductive manner

"It was his weekend off. He can do what he wants. Do you spend time with your girlfriend? Do you go to the cinema with her? Would you like her to kiss you now and then? That's what Artur [Boruc] has done. I still go to the cinema with my wife and still kiss her. She doesn't like it, but there you go."

The Celtic manager after his goalkeeper was spotted out in town

"It's embarrassing, I'm not proud of it. I can't even make myself anything to eat. I had to phone her and she said, 'I've left something to put in the microwave'. An hour later and I'm asking, 'Where's the microwave?'"

Getting cooking tips from his wife

"I'm afraid that this is me getting on my high horse now. But we have yob television, yob newspapers, and funny enough, whereas it was my mum and dad, school, police, church who used to set the standards, now it's tabloids and yob television who set the standards by which people live."

Strachan gives his thoughts on society

"You shouldn't be seen drunk as a football player, it's not on. If you want to get drunk, lock yourself in the house. If you're getting 100 times more than the average wage, it's celebrity status and you're there to be picked on. If you want to be a celebrity, stick yourself on the celebrity pages. But if you want to be a footballer, be a footballer."

The Coventry boss on drinking culture

"It is always fun getting attacked – one of the highlights of my career. He got fined £100 for that but they got a whip-round in the pub and he got £200."

After being assaulted by a Celtic fan while an Aberdeen player

OH GORD!

"I became so angry with a mate of mine on the golf course, that I didn't speak to him for seven holes. For those seven holes I played even par golf."

He's more focused when angry

"If there's anyone luckier than a footballer, it's a footballer's wife. She has all the money and prestige but none of the pressure."

The Saints manager's view on WAGs

"We even competed for the acne cream when we were younger. Obviously I won that one!"

Strachan on his former Aberdeen teammate Alex McLeish

"For years they've been clamouring on about getting the same money as Italians or Spaniards. Now they've got it, they should behave like them. You cannot go and drink on a Tuesday and Wednesday but stay in on a Friday. That's no good. You have to stay in all week now."

The Coventry chief on booze control

"I've got a local pub I go to on a Saturday night about half past nine and everybody there knows absolutely zero about football. So whether you win 7-0 or lose 7-0 you go and talk about who's been doing what in the village."

The boss values down-time at Coventry

OH GORD!

MANAGING JUST FINE

"I wouldn't put my house on it. I've worked too hard for 35 years to risk that."

When asked if Celtic can win 2-0 at Barcelona

"I just went along to see him, to see how many times he was caught offside – and he didn't let me down."

The Celtic boss explains why he watched Norwich's friendly against Falkirk – it wasn't to sign Darren Huckerby

"24's on. Jack Bauer, he's some man. Wouldn't mind him in the back four!"

When asked what he's doing that night to celebrate Celtic's 2006 title success

"It's dangerous to try and fight him [Alex Ferguson] when you've got a sponge and he's armed with a machine gun."

On fighting the famous 'hairdryer'

"An agent said to me once that you have to blindfold a player and gag them to get them up here – then put a big wad in their pocket. So it's definitely not easy."

On the challenges of getting players to move north of the border

"We hope it could be Yao Ming on the football pitch here."

Erm, OK then!

"There will not be any foreigners coming in this time, that's for sure. We have to add that wee bit of enthusiasm and knowledge."

The Boro boss wants to evoke a British spirit

"I've seen [Shunsuke] Nakamura and had a laugh about it. I peek round the corner when he's doing his weights and sing 'Cheerio, Cheerio'."

On reports the midfielder is being lured away

"I went in for contract talks with Bill and came out with three season tickets and owing the club money."

On Leeds chairman Bill Fotherby

"The transfer list thing went out in the 1970s, it doesn't happen here so it's a mysterious one. I was having a cup of tea and a rhubarb tart when I saw it and I nearly spluttered."

He responds to speculation that Kenny Miller had been transfer listed

"It is 10 past 11 on my watch. It is funny when somebody asks me how long is to go on a Saturday. I just wanted a reminder that when I get ideas above my station, how football can kick you in the guts."

He still wears the watch that stopped during Celtic's 5-0 Champions League defeat to Artmedia Bratislava

"I've never been to a board meeting in my life. My chairman will pop into my house for a cup of tea and a blether. We do our own thing, which is rare."

The Coventry boss on his good relationship

"We'll try and win because we're not clever enough to try anything else."

Ahead of Southampton's UEFA Cup tie with Steaua Bucharest

"We're actually trying to sign Snow White to lead my players out at Old Trafford. If we can get hold of her, we might be all right."

The Celtic manager on his dwarf-like side

"I had a call the other day from an agent who wanted to sell me a Cameroonian centre forward. I told him, no. He said, 'But you don't even know his name'. I told him I've got two forwards who made the England squad this season. I've got [Viorel] Moldovan at the World Cup with Romania. And I've got two lads I can't even give a game to. I don't need to know his name."

The Coventry manager's issue with agents

"When I'm dead, it will be inscribed on my headstone: 'This isn't as bad as that night in Bratislava'."

After Celtic's 5-0 Champions League defeat by Artmedia Bratislava

Interviewer: "What about Rangers getting to the UEFA Cup Final?"

Celtic's Strachan: "I have no problem, we couldn't get the chance to beat them. We weren't in their competition!"

"I'm not saying you have to be married to be a good footballer. I'm just saying it felt strange to come to a club where there are only three members of the first-team squad who are married. You need responsibility in life. I'm not going about finding wives for them, it was just a shock to me."

On the lack of commitment from his Middlesbrough players

"They don't have to eat it. They can eat or go hungry."

The Coventry manager after changing the food 'dramatically' at the training ground

"I might start panicking tonight, take a drink and become an alcoholic. But the TV is alright tonight, so we should be OK."

When asked about the threat of Rangers

"If I turn the telly on at 7.30 on a Sunday morning, there's some bird with long blonde hair telling me how I should run my team."

The Coventry boss referring to Soccer AM's Helen Chamberlain

"If you come in smelling of drink on a Thursday, you're not playing on a Saturday. I'll not fine you, but I'll say, 'You can explain it to the press why you're not playing, explain to the fans, these people who give you all that money, how you've been disrespectful to the people you play with'."

The Coventry boss has zero tolerance

"My toes are like horrible wee bits and bobs. It scares people on the beach as I walk along in my thong."

Strachan had his toe nails pulled out by the roots as it was causing him trouble

"We are trying hard to bring in people who can lead... I want to bring in leaders and men – that's hugely important now. I have to have people who I know, players I know who are men, who are leaders."

The Middlesbrough manager doesn't want followers... or women

"You try to talk to them nicely, but it doesn't always sink in. Eventually you go whack them right across the backside and that keeps them away from the flames."

On getting the most out of his Celtic players

"Time was when the budget at Celtic was the fourth or fifth biggest in British football. Nowadays we're finding we can't compete for wages with the likes of Hull City!"

On the financial constraints at Celtic

"I've got a five-year contract. If I last five years it will be an absolute miracle."

During his time as Coventry manager

"It's also reassuring to know that 50 per cent of males over 60 tonight have been out with my wife."

Strachan lights up an after-dinner talk

"It's good to see Shaun [Maloney] and John [Kennedy] back training. It's fantastic they both got back on the same week because it means they don't have to split up at any time whatsoever. Now they're called the Twins, after the film with Danny DeVito and Arnold Schwarzenegger."

The boss is happy his Celtic duo are finally back fit again

"It's not a couple of fans I have to keep happy... I have to keep millions happy, I mean millions in the world, you do not understand what it feels like."

The pressures of managing Celtic

"I had to take him into my house for six weeks because the police said to me, 'If he gets picked up again, he's going to jail'. So I said to my wife, 'We're having a guest'. She said, 'Who is it?' I said, 'Noel Whelan'. She said 'Jesus'."

On dealing with controversial striker Noel Whelan at Coventry

"There have been more sightings of the Loch Ness monster."

On Saints striker Agustin Delgado, who had made four starts in three years, and was often seen back home in Ecuador

"The games they play on television, they'll be turning the volume up just a wee bit to make it louder."

Strachan believes Sky Sports turn up the volume for dramatic effect when teams are being booed

"Our midfield has about one goal between them in the last year. Did you see David Prutton's effort at Everton last week? We needed air traffic clearance."

The Southampton boss on his goal-shy midfield

OH GORD!

OTHERS ON STRACHAN

"He was playing from memory – but by God what a memory!"

Ron Atkinson on midfielder Strachan coming back from injury at Man United

"He can destroy at once the big tough guys in the dressing room with one lash of his coruscating tongue. That's why he earned the nickname 'King Tongue'."

Howard Wilkinson on his former player

"There's nobody fitter at his age – except maybe Raquel Welch."

Atkinson on his veteran Coventry star

"I wouldn't want to expose my back to him in a hurry."

Sir Alex Ferguson is certainly not a fan

Reporter: "Do you see any of yourself in Gordon Strachan?"

Alex Ferguson: "I don't think so. I hope not."

"At least I can go on a diet. What is he going to do about the colour of his hair and his silly voice?"

Thurrock boss Colin McBride after Strachan said he was slightly overweight on TV

"After a year in charge, we had not improved one iota – the football was average, away results were abysmal, the worst league position in 20 years and he still doesn't know his best team. It wasn't just on the field that Strachan let himself down, off the field during post-match interviews he became an embarrassment to himself, the club and the fans. He was arrogant, obnoxious, sarcastic, cutting and rude. He came across to me like a man who was on the borderline of insanity."

An epic rant from ex-Middlesborough star Bernie Slavin on Strachan's stint as manager

"It's getting to him... just look at him next time he's on TV. He never looks at the interviewer and comes out with baffling gibberish. The cameraman deserves a bonus for keeping his head in the frame."

Brian Clough on the Coventry boss

"When Gordon came to Leeds, I was only 18 and he opened my eyes. He was supposed to be past it but I was amazed at how he lived his life. He even ate seaweed."

Gary Speed on his former teammate

Also available

Made in the USA
Monee, IL
07 December 2019

18151010R00066